*Quick*GUIDES
everything you need to know...fast

DIRECT MAIL FUNDRAISING

By John Baguley

reviewed by Graham McKern

WIREMILL
PUBLISHING LTD

Across the world the organizations and institutions that fundraise to finance their work are referred to in many different ways. They are charities, non-profits or not-for-profit organizations, non-governmental organizations (NGOs), voluntary organizations, academic institutions, agencies, etc. For ease of reading, we have used the term Nonprofit Organization, Organization or NPO as an umbrella term throughout the *Quick*Guide series. We have also used the spellings and punctuation used by the author.

Published by
Wiremill Publishing Ltd.
Edenbridge, Kent TN8 5PS, UK
info@wiremillpublishing.com
www.wiremillpublishing.com
www.quickguidesonline.com

British Library Cataloguing in Publication Data
A catalogue record for this book is available from the British Library.

ISBN Number 1-905053-31-2

Printed by Rhythm Consolidated Berhad, Malaysia
Cover Design by Jennie de Lima and Edward Way
Design by Colin Woodman Design

CONTENTS

INTRODUCTION

I once lived in a small fishing village. When a boat hit the rocks or sank, people ran through the village asking passers-by for help. They then knocked on the doors of relatives and later phoned people living farther away to seek their assistance for the widows and orphans. Later still, they wrote to people who had moved away or who lived overseas.

Direct mail is the last of these natural actions, yet it can reach the most people and build powerful organisations. It is also a very flexible medium and can be targeted to just a few people with a very personal approach. Indeed, the more personal any letter is, the more likely it is to succeed.

It will work in every country where there is a mail service.

This Guide will take you through the whole direct mail process step by step. Always remember, however, that direct mail is only a letter from one person to another, asking that individual to kindly help someone in distress, and then making it easy for him or her to give money. People will give to help others, not to meet your organisation's needs.

Direct mail is used for four main fundraising purposes:
- Recruit new supporters.
- Ask supporters to give additional funds.
- Move people from ad hoc to committed and regular giving.
- Invite people to attend events or take part in other activities.

This guide covers the first three purposes. It concentrates on mass mailings, though the key principles also apply if you are writing to only a few people.

Reviewer's Comment

Direct mail describes mail that is addressed to a particular addressee, for example, Mr. John Smith. Indirect mail, on the other hand, is mail that is addressed only to a category of addressees, for example, The Home Owner or Concerned Citizen.

Raising Funds by Mail

Direct mail is a useful part of the fundraiser's arsenal of methods of acquiring new supporters and donors, communicating with current supporters, and increasing the involvement by current supporters in your organisation.

Following are the steps for a successful direct mail campaign.

- Know why you are holding the campaign. Are you seeking new members or communicating with current supporters? Are the costs appropriate for the return you expect?

- Know how this mailing fits into your overall fundraising or communication strategy. Is this a planned mailing within a series? Is this in response to an emergency? Is the communication in response to a major campaign or one-time need?

- If you will be communicating with current supporters, do you have an adequate database of information about your current supporters? Will you be able to mail to segments of your supporters, such as major donors? Do you need to obtain more information about donors or ensure the information is in place for the next mailing?

- Do you have the capability within your organisation to write and design the mailing, or do you need to obtain professional help or volunteers with specific expertise?

- Do you have the capability within your organisation to merge the information from your database into the letters or other material that you are going to send?

- Do you plan to send additional brochures or other materials in the mailing? Has that been organised and available when needed?

- Can you handle stuffing the envelopes yourself or should you use a mailing house?

- Have you put in place the systems to thank donors?

One reason for the mailing may be to recruit new donors, in this case the most important factor is getting your target audience right. You can write the most brilliant letter in the world, but if you send it to the wrong list of people, no one will write back except to complain and ask where you obtained their address.

Think about your current donors. People who are similar to your existing supporters are most likely to be your future supporters. Indeed, if you have enough supporters, send them a lifestyle questionnaire and find out just what they are really like. For example, are they male or female? How old are they? How do they vote? Which newspapers and magazines do they read? What are their interests, hobbies? People will love to tell you about themselves, and if the questionnaire is anonymous, they will answer almost any question.

Many countries have list brokers who will sell you lists of people (called "cold" lists because they are unknown to you) which are divided into different demographics, such as age, sex, wealth. If there are none available, you will need to be creative and look for lists of appropriate names and addresses.

Reviewer's Comment
"List buying" is the term used to describe obtaining the names and addresses of people who fit the specific target criteria you have requested. Often lists are acquired for one mailing only, rather than bought outright. This might be a less expensive option.

Also think about professional associations, residents' committees, unions and social groups, readers, and buyers of professional products. Look for people who have some disposable income, may already shop by mail, and are in caring professions. Direct mail has even successfully been sent to people listed in telephone directories in countries where those people were wealthy enough to afford phones, had been residents in their homes for four or five years and could receive follow-up calls to letters.

Reviewer's Comment
In some countries, using the telephone directory as a source for names and addresses will breach copyright laws. It is best to check with your local direct marketing industry association on copyright-free sources for obtaining names and addresses or, alternatively, to buy or hire lists based on your needs, if possible.

When you acquire a list, remember to check it against your own list of supporters – you need to be careful not to mail your current members to ask them to join again.

Also remember that people are increasingly receiving unsolicited mail. It is incumbent on your organisation to not increase that burden unnecessarily. Ensure you carefully target people who might be interested in your cause.

RECIPROCAL MAILINGS

One way of attracting new donors is through reciprocal mailings with other organisations. With reciprocal mailings, you mail your supporters another organisation's package, and that organisation mails its supporters an equal number of your packages. That way, your list of names does not leave your control.

In some countries, there is a well-organised system of reciprocal mailings to like-minded organisations that keeps this activity within the local data protection law. Those engaging in a reciprocal mailing usually need to inform their supporters (at the point of acquiring their names and addresses) that this is an activity of the organisation. Sometimes supporters must be given the chance to opt into or out of that programme. Data protection law tends to disapprove of reciprocal mailings, so ensure that this is within your local laws.

In many countries, the return on direct mail is now so low that, for many only reciprocal mailings actually earn a profit in the first year or two. Where there is less competition, the returns can be much higher. Philanthropic people tend to realise that there are many organisations whose work they would like to support, and they begin to build a portfolio of supported NPOs, much like investing in a range of stocks and shares.

Ensure that you exchange the same number of names and that you exchange lists of lapsed supporters separately, and also think about excluding your most generous supporters from the list. Sometimes organisations ask for lists of people who have given over a certain amount. Consider that each of these factors affects the response rate and/or the average gift.

Another use for direct mail is to communicate with current donors. Donors love you most when they have just made their first donation. You have the glow of the honeymoon in which to translate that affection into a lifelong relationship. Try sending a small welcome pack with information about how they can get involved in your organisation and include a return coupon on which they can indicate their interest by marking what they would like to do. Include an envelope with your address already on it so they can easily return the form. If you can have the envelope prepaid, so much the better. Making a response very easy is a key theme of direct mail.

Use direct mail to keep in touch with current supporters. Asking your supporters (a "warm" list) to make an extra donation or to sign up for a regular donation is a time when you can be creative and imaginative. Each time you write, elaborate on and tell a story about a different part of your organisation's work, or about the environment or animals that you may be protecting. At some time in the letter, the reader should have an emotional response: "Oh no, I must do something to help." Think carefully about how you will trigger that reaction.

Do not ask for money to buy computers or overheads – ask for funds to help extend your work or mission.

Often the best time to mail is after the end-of-year celebrations, which is traditionally a quiet time. Direct mail is a medium which requires reflective reading by the recipient to work best. In many countries, the build-up to the year-end, or other religious celebrations, is a good time to appeal as people are reminded that they should care for those less well-off than themselves. This is often the time of the "annual appeal," when supporters are encouraged to renew their gifts. Stay away from known holiday, or vacation, periods; instead of coming home to read their accumulated mail at their leisure, people dispose of as much of it as fast as possible.

Reviewer's Comment
It is often worth asking for larger gifts at the end of a financial year if donations to your organisation attract a tax benefit. This practice is common in some countries.

Continues on next page

Establishing a regular pattern of appeals will both set a pattern for your supporters and ensure they are not approached more often by your rivals. The rule is to increase the number of your appeals until they are no longer profitable.

In between these appeals for additional funds, it is customary to send a newsletter so that supporters become much more knowledgeable about your organisation and the good work their donations are achieving. Organisations often send out four newsletters in a year as well as four separate appeals. In some countries, these can be increased to six of both.

Remember, your supporters only know about you through the newsletter and the appeals. It is the appeals that really move them and reaffirm their commitment, even if they do not give each time.

Encouraging Regular Giving

Another use of direct mail is to seek regular gifts from donors and thus reduce the need for constant appeals. The process of sending repeated appeals is cumbersome, and it is easier if you can induce your supporters to set up regular donations to you if possible. Because people are sometimes paid monthly, it is much easier for them to pay a small sum per month than to give a large annual gift. The benefit of this approach is that people go on paying year after year and rarely cancel, unless you upset them or they lose their jobs.

Many organisations owe their survival to committed giving. When all else has failed them, the regular payments have kept them going, providing core income to meet their office and basic staff costs. It takes hard work, however, to bring between, say, 30 percent and 60 percent of your supporters into this form of giving. I would advocate devoting one appeal per year to such "upgrading," stressing just how important it is for those whom you are helping to have the stability that this form of giving brings.

To those who sign up for regular giving, do not make the mistake of promising that you'll never send future appeals. People will miss the drama of the appeals and give to other organisations instead, thinking you are becoming inactive.

Offer people a range of giving options. Your supporters are likely to have widely differing incomes and could well give more than you might imagine. It is hard to think like someone who earns much more money than you do, but if you can meet and chat with your richer supporters, for even a few minutes, you may learn a lot that will help your fundraising.

Direct mail is a wonderful medium with which to raise funds because you can contact thousands of people at one time while treating each person almost individually. This means you can ask different donors for different types or amounts of donations.

This is where the information you hold about donors is crucial. A database or electronic list will help you or your mailing agency separate donors and send them the appropriate letter, package or offer.

You do not want to offend wealthy or committed donors by asking for too little. You also do not want to scare away donors with fewer resources or with a tenuous commitment to your organisation. One option is simply to send out different reply coupons, some with suggested donations that are relatively small and some with suggested donations that are large. If skillfully done, this option can greatly increase your income from appeals, and you can have several different levels of giving if the division between your richer and poorer supporters is quite high.

A more sophisticated approach is to form separate clubs to which people can belong. Each club has its own level of donation and its own rewards. For example, a zoo may have the Keepers Club where donors receive a special discount card for the zoo shop and admittance at certain times when the zoo is normally closed, plus the possibility of feeding and grooming certain animals. The zoo may also have a Presidents Club where donors give at an even higher rate; as well as having the privileges of the Keepers Club, they also meet the president, chief executive officer and animal keepers at an annual dinner and are invited to attend an exclusive early view of new animals and certain births.

Thinking through this kind of club structure for your organisation can create a powerful bond with potential major donors and allow an interaction that will create opportunities for major gifts.

THANKING YOUR DONORS

For donors, little is as rewarding as prompt sincere thanks for their gift. Equally, little is as off-putting as not being thanked, or receiving a thank-you letter months after they made a gift. After all, didn't you need the money? Your direct mail campaign doesn't end when the envelopes go into the mail. It is a continual process whereby a person who responds to a direct mail pack is properly thanked, appropriately involved in your organisation, and valued throughout the relationship.

You've written to potential donors and spent your organisation's funds to tell them about your organisation and solicit their support. They have responded as you had hoped. Now you need to respond as they hope. Come to an agreement on which part of your organisation will send the thank-you letters. Will it be your finance department where the cheques arrive, or your membership department when they log the members and donors, or the fundraising department that organised the mailing? I prefer a computerised thank-you from the finance department accompanied by a letter written by the fundraising or membership department.

This thank-you letter should vary along with the appeal and be different each time someone gives. Write the thank-you letter when you write the appeal letter and have it signed by the same person who signed the appeal letter. That way the process is believable.

People who donate by direct mail are said to be "direct mail responsive." This means they are likely to also respond to further appeals and read newsletters. It may also be that they will respond to telephone calls and invitations to events or buy lottery tickets, but that needs to be tested and not assumed.

The real value of a supporter is over his or her lifetime. To keep supporters on board, they need to be given the opportunity to see the work and take part in the organisation's activities, if at all possible.

Do treat supporters who have been with the organisation a long time as old friends, perhaps inviting them to "open days" when they can meet the director and staff and learn more about your work.

You may decide that an agency can help you identify and manage the lists of people to whom you want to send your mailing.

In the early days of building a database of supporters, it is usual to undertake much of the work in-house, unless you are particularly well funded. Listing everyone who contacts you in any way, sending out a newsletter once or twice a year, and a simple appeal letter toward the end of each year are customary.

At some stage, you will want to expand and bring in hundreds or thousands of new supporters. This can only be done with professional help either in-house or through an agency. The advantage of using an agency is that you will have a range of expertise at your disposal, which will enable you to compete with other organisations in list buying, copywriting, design, printing and mailing efficiency. An agency will also produce, or help you produce, significant statistics with which you can judge the effectiveness of the programme.

All this comes at a cost. With returns from direct mail gradually falling in many countries, choosing the right agency is crucial. Skills are transferable from one nonprofit organisation (NPO) to another, so do not just choose an agency that has worked for a similar organisation, but look for outstanding work done for any NPO. Try to be neither the smallest nor the largest organisation that the agency has on its books. Do take up references, but also check exactly who or which team will be working on your account.

You should always consider at least three agencies, but do not ask them to produce sample material specifically for your organisation. This is expensive and time-consuming for them, which means smaller agencies cannot compete. Do discuss list buying as much as creative work because they may have access to lists which you have not seen or information you haven't considered.

Using a Mailing House

Once you have decided to communicate by direct mail (for whatever reason), you will need to decide whether to send out your mailing yourself or use a professional company.

Do you know the cost of mailing, how long a mailing takes and the opportunities for discounts in your country? It is wise to start by checking the conditions of your mail service. You can usually obtain a discount for large-scale mailings, especially if you provide the mail to the postal service in whatever order it requires for such special price, for example, in postcode or zip code order. A special requirement of the postal service may include the use of your return address on each envelope so unopened letters can be given back to you. This is a benefit to you which tells you who has moved or refused your mail. It also allows you to "clean" your list by removing these names.

If you are using a mailing house, it will advise you on these details. Mailing houses receive the separate parts of your mailing (for example, the outer envelope, letter, leaflet, return coupon and return envelope) and put them all together in your outer envelope. They will stamp and deliver the envelope to the mail service in order to receive the best price for the mailing. Mailing houses or printers may also "mail-merge" your letters. This means they receive your list of supporters or potential supporters, either electronically or on sticky labels, and print or affix these to your letters. These are then usually placed in a "window envelope" with the address on the letter showing through the clear window. (Other ideas for the outer envelope and letter are covered later.)

Earlier, your printer will have prepared the outer envelope and printed any information you want on the front (for example, "Urgent – please help today") and the return address, usually on the back, as well as the letters, return coupon and return envelope.

Of course, any of these stages from print to delivery can be, and often are, done in-house. You can stuff up to 1,000 envelopes a day and use ordinary postage stamps and handwritten additions to letters wherever that is possible. For really large mailings, the cost per letter is minimal if you use professional firms.

THE ENVELOPE

Size of Envelope
The outer envelope gives the first impression of your direct mail package, which is often the size of a single sheet of standard letterhead-sized paper that has been folded into thirds. However, using a larger envelope can make your mailing stand out and look well worth opening. It can be as large as is appropriate for the contents. This is the first option you need to address.

Windows or Not
Window envelopes are typically used because mailing houses find it almost impossible to match addresses on the letters to the corresponding personalised envelopes. If one envelope is missed, the entire print run will be off and the wrong letter will go into the wrong envelope.

Text or Picture
A line of text and perhaps a picture help separate your envelope from other mass mailings, inducing people to open it. Read a lot of other organisations' mail before doing this in order to choose text that will not just encourage the recipient to throw away the letter unopened.

Return Address
Your address should be written somewhere on the envelope so returned mail can be sent to you. Then you can tell how up-to-date your list is and correct your own records that generated the list.

If you are mailing to supporters in another country, it is a good idea to provide a local (same country) return address (for example, you can use local staff, volunteers or even an embassy address). Few people like to send money out of their country, and the mail service will rarely return mail to you from a different country.

Stamps or Not
Ask your mail service about discounts for a mass mailing. For very short runs, however, consider individual stamps and handwritten envelopes. Some printers' computers can produce "handwriting" that is now excellent and should be considered, though I would not use it for the whole letter.

Class

If you have a two-tier mail system, it is rarely worth the cost of using the faster mail, such as first class. If you are mailing to major donors or committed supporters, however, do consider special edition or other premium stamps.

Colour

The colour of the envelope is usually white, but you can choose any colour that will work in your country and be appropriate for the content of your mailing.

At each stage of designing your direct mail pack, there are two trade-offs: One is getting your pack noticed versus having it look like a personal communication; the other is the efficiency of mass production versus the personal touch.

Reviewer's Comment

While mailing houses use "intelligent bar coding" to keep multiple pages together for the one donor, it cannot be used on outer envelopes because it can conflict with mail-sorting bar codes used in some countries by the postal service to deliver mail.

THE LETTER

The Letter is simple. It says what the problem or need is in human terms, tells how it could be solved with the recipient's help, and encourages the recipient to give and/or get involved. Most direct mail letters are one or two sides of letter-sized paper. The more you write, the more effective it can be but only if each paragraph is effective. You can lose the reader at any weak paragraph in several pages of text.

Underlining, bold text, different-coloured text or different fonts are best discarded or used very sparingly. The letter must read like a normal letter.

The letter should come from a person of significance in the organisation whom the reader will know or from the director. One person should sign it, and the return envelope should go back to that person. Your supporters also should come to know the particular writer through your newsletters and your appeals. The writer should have a passion for the work and care deeply about the problem you are trying to solve.

Continues on next page

If the mailing is going to individuals who have not yet been supporters of the organisation, identify who they would most like to hear from in your organisation. Is it the chief executive? A volunteer? A current supporter?

Do not use jargon and do not assume the readers know much about the things you care about, but do not try to educate them. Speak to the readers as intelligent and kind human beings – your newsletters will educate them later.

Don't forget to ask for a donation; for example, "Please help us by making a donation today." The "today" is important. Each appeal should have a sense of urgency if it is to be seen as important. "Please reply by ... because we need to know how much we can spend to ..."

Incentives in letters inviting donations (where donors receive something if they join or donate) work well if they are appropriate. An incentive such as a special pen or book from an organisation encouraging literacy can be used to encourage large gifts; smaller items (a cheap pen, cards or small address labels) can help encourage the recipient to open the letter. The latter is typical of some large-scale mailings, particularly those seeking small donations.

Reviewer's Comment

Care needs to be taken, in some countries, not to offer a gift or other incentive to solicit donations. In some countries, that practice may invalidate tax benefits for the donation.

P.S.

Everyone reads the P.S., even if they read nothing else in the letter – use it.

The best thing about direct mail is that you can test every option by splitting the mailing and coding each return coupon separately so you know the result. Will your chairman's or director's signature work better on the letter? Test it!

Reviewer's Comment

If you're testing the mailing by sending different things to different recipients, make sure you only change one variable. If you change more than one variable, the results become inconclusive and you won't know what caused the difference in results. Was it the person who signed the letter that made the difference? Was it because you added a graphic image of a starving child?

ADDITIONAL MATERIAL

What do your readers need to know to make a decision? A small leaflet is often added to give the opportunity for some visuals and text to introduce the organisation more fully. You need to tell recipients what they might want to know, not what you want them to know – make sure you know the difference.

The other frequent addition to direct mail is a "lift letter." This is an additional letter, written by someone whom the readers will respect. The letter writer confirms that he or she supports the appeal, and your organisation is trustworthy and carries out the work it says it does. This is not a letter from an eminent person in your organisation's field of work, whom the readers might never have heard of, but maybe a nationally known patron who is in the press and on television.

At different times, you can add large booklets, cards to be signed and returned with a donation, CDs and pens. Each item must have a specific reason for being included that links to the text in your letter and reinforces the appeal. Additional items can be a distraction and may also push your package into a new weight and cost band, so you must be clear about the merits before adding them to the mix.

A frequent addition is a campaigning card which is something for the recipient to send on to a member of the government on behalf of your organisation's work. This is an attempt to add value to the fundraising pack by making it more than just an appeal for donations; people can choose the soft option and just send the card on (and you are, in effect, saying that this is just as good as making a donation). If you do wish to add a campaigning card which is sent on, you can add a box which the recipient can mark to indicate a donation was also made to your organisation. On the coupon

Continues on next page

which is returned to you, add a box to mark which states, "I have today sent a postcard to Y." This way, people may be more likely to send the card on as well as make a donation.

THE RETURN COUPON

The return coupon is a wonderful device. You will know exactly who sent it because you can print the person's name as well as his or her address onto both the letter and the coupon at the same time. This is why many letters have the coupon attached – it makes the printing process simple.

Coupons without a pre-printed address need to leave a lot of space for those with poor handwriting and for the elderly whose vision is often restricted. Always ask people to write in capital letters. Adding "Mr/Ms/Mrs/Other" will tell you the gender of your supporters and enable you to effectively personalise your future letters to them.

Code each coupon so that you know which list it was sent to, and don't forget to put the code on each supporter's record so you know how he or she was identified (if new to the organisation) or what appeal was

responded to (if a current supporter). Remember to keep a list of the codes and what they mean!

Do reaffirm the gift by putting a sentence on the coupon such as, "Yes, I would like to help prevent Z and make a donation of Y." Then add a row of boxes with a range of corresponding monetary amounts, so the person may choose which amount to give. Most people read these from left to right and stop at their comfort zone, so start with the highest amounts on the left to increase your average donation. Many people mark the middle box, so ensure there is a large range. Do put "Other" at the right so readers can add their own amount.

Many people pay by credit card, and it is worth listing the different types of cards you accept. Also be sure to clearly indicate the name to which cheques should be written.

Suggest a date by which the recipient should reply. When determining the date, remember that it takes time for the whole process of printing, packing and mailing letters before the recipient receives the letter. When setting suggested reply dates, do ensure there is enough time for the whole process to be completed, at least two weeks for the recipient to decide and time for the coupon to come back to you.

THE RETURN ENVELOPE

The return envelope, if it is stamped and pre-addressed, will greatly increase your successful returns. This way, your supporters will not need to search for a stamp or your address.

Find out how you can prepay postage. The best option is if you only need to pay for envelopes that are actually sent back to you. The worst option is to have to pay to stamp each reply envelope regardless of whether it is used. In the first situation, however, it is customary to say, "You do not need to use a stamp, but if you do, it will save us postage." Often a third of respondents will do this, and in a large mailing, this will save you money.

Remember to make sure the return coupon fits easily into the return envelope and both fit into the original envelope!

The name on the return envelope should be that of the person who signed the letter, so people feel that their money is going to the right place.

Return envelopes are usually a different colour from the outer envelope.

When you are mailing to several lists, testing various ideas and receiving large sums of money through the mail, it is important to keep a clear record of costs and income from each list and each test. This is a record of both the number of replies and the average donation from each list or segment of that list. (For example, you could be testing three ideas in one list, each with a different code.)

It is customary, when first starting to use certain direct mail lists, to buy only a limited part of a list, and only if that limited part gives you the result you need to "roll out," or mail to, the whole list.

So you need an accounting package or grid that will handle this level of detail and allow you to make a prediction. You need to ask yourself: "If we take this direct mail and roll it out to these other lists, without the additional agency costs of creating any more new packages, then what will be the result?" One way of looking at this result is in terms of "return on investment," or ROI. This will tell you how much you will get back for each unit of currency invested for each list. Of course, if the number of members is more important than the amount of money, then that number per unit of currency will be your ROI.

If you are using an agency to handle your direct mail, then their fees will be a key factor, but remember that their overall costs are likely to go down in time. Once you have found the best design, you will not be creating any new packages for a year or two.

If the agency is handling your appeals, then each appeal will be a new package; that way, your supporters will treat each appeal as a special ask, not just as a routine reminder appeal. Data protection laws now often affect the way you acquire, hold and use searchable lists of people's names and addresses. These laws vary from country to country but generally are new and often untested in the courts. Do avoid becoming a test case by reading the law and following it scrupulously – if you are in doubt, seek legal advice.

DATA PROTECTION AND PRIVACY

The law is often based on principles; it is wise to follow them regardless of their legal status. For example, if you keep data on people, that information should be safe from access by someone who might use that data in a way the person(s) would find objectionable. Locks on filing cabinets and access codes on computers are the usual safety measures. When you first ask people to join or donate to your organisation, they should know what that entails, that is, how their names and addresses will be used. Will they be sent a regular newsletter or email? Will you or other organisations ask them for additional donations? Will their names and addresses be sold to a commercial company or other organisation?

Data protection is largely common sense, but the law is often complex and you must understand it before you ask people to donate and give you their addresses, not least because many of them could be lawyers. Without the address, however, you cannot ask for additional donations, and your direct mail programme is very likely to fail financially.

CONCLUSION

In many ways, direct mail is the easiest way to raise funds – you only need to sit down and write a letter. Indeed, the most successful direct mail appeals read as if someone had just heard of the problem and written the appeal to a friend for help.

Direct mail allows you to present your case to thousands of people cheaply and quickly, in a way that lets them take the time to consider the merits of your approach.

Given an efficient mail service, an effective banking system, computerised databases and good printing facilities, direct mail will work anywhere.

Direct mail can provide you with a long-term source of core income. Because it is based on a great many people giving, it is a sustainable system unlike funds from government, industry or grantmaking bodies that can change their objectives and funding patterns from one year to another.

If you haven't tested it for your NPO, try it now. Remember, the thousands of people who did not respond have learnt about your organisation and its work. They may respond next time or the time after that.